The Collie of Carneddau

The Collie of Carneddau

by

Richard Moon

Table of Contents

INTRODUCTION

'A dog is a man's best friend.' Naturally, they are everyone's best friend and that must be the case where millions of dogs are concerned. Our dog is my best friend, the best friend I've ever had. We all experience and appreciate that powerful bond we get through having a dog, or any pet. Everyone can be inspired by their own pet to tell a story about how their companion has enriched their and their family's lives.

Everyone has a favourite place. For some it's by the sea, for others it's the top of a hill. Life is full of highs and lows. Like I keep telling the dog — 'It's all downhill from here.'

A brief, light hearted look at the life of a dog — in and around the Welsh Three Thousands of the Carneddau. It is a narrow, bias view of the area and doesn't attempt to cover all the beautiful locations like a good guide book would do. Besides not claiming to be an expert dog trainer, I am not an expert writer, walker or climber either. Experienced — but no expert.

Is it a guide book about walks in North Wales or a Border Collie owner's manual offering advice on how not to rear a dog? It's none of them. It's more like a pamphlet, or souvenir brochure — with amazing pictures and few words. To be enjoyed in conjunction with a better map than the one provided.

WARNING! This document may require you to have a great sense of humour.

See next page for our crude, rough, route map.

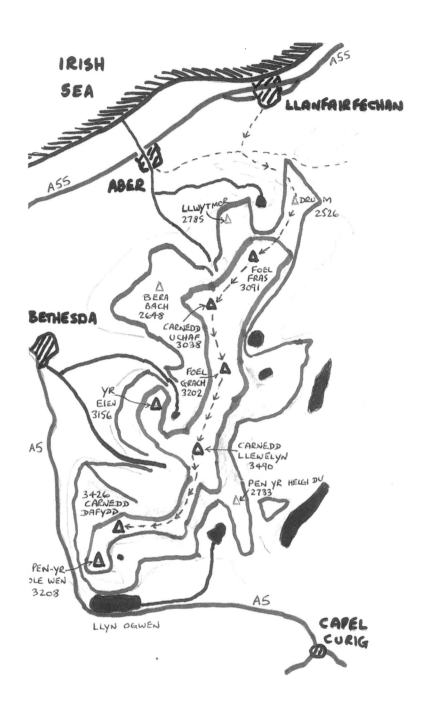

IRISH SEA

ASS

LLANFAIRFECHAN

ASS

ABER

LLWYTMOR
2785

DRUM
2526

FOEL
FRAS
3091

BERA
BACH
2648

CARNEDD
UCHAF
3038

BETHESDA

FOEL
GRACH
3202

YR
ELEN
3156

A5

CARNEDD
LLEWELYN
3490

PEN YR HELGI DU
2733

3426
CARNEDD
DAFYDD

PEN-YR-
OLE WEN
3208

A5

LLYN OGWEN

CAPEL
CURIG

2

THE COLLIE

I would never have entertained getting a dog, but now all I seem to do is try to keep the dog entertained. He wasn't my idea and I don't take responsibility for the way he has worked out. I am his keeper, not his coach. I am only looking after him for someone else.

That critical phase has been missed when he would have been most receptive to learning and he has used that time instead learning the joys of doing what he wants. Collies are capable of learning the wrong things just as rapidly as the right ones. So we won't be entering him into competitions just yet.

Cisco, resting on the slopes of Foel Fras

He has a fear of almost everything, so needy and insecure. His pet hate is the local golf course, the sound of the club hitting the ball. Cars with purposely loud exhausts and motorbikes do the same to him. Worst of all are those contraptions which are meant to scare birds which sound like a gunshot, or a starting pistol – a car door shutting sounds very similar – causing panic in his mind. You couldn't even tempt him with a steak at such times. He will try to run away with no clear plan of where he is going. Does he ever stop to think what's it all about?

We have a book which lists all the things a good collie should be and you can't even tick one thing off that's on the list. He is the exact opposite of what he should be. Having said this he is still a clever collie. Good dog breeders, experts, or those who think they are experts, would look down their noses at all this, but there is a light hearted side to this failure which should be enjoyed. Yes the dog is ruined, but there is still so much joy to express regarding his personality and friendship that makes him special in the eyes of those close to him. To capture that personality and put it into words, his expressions, the look in his eyes and that raising of the eyebrow – is not that easy to do.

He is quite anti-social and I don't know if that is indicative of the mentality of his keeper or not. He has to be protected from himself by carefully managing his encounters with other people and other dogs. He is so unpredictable. Border Collies have it all – they have good looks, intelligence and high trainability. Well Cisco has 'up to', (as they say in broadband lingo) two of those attributes. When certain dogs approach us while out walking he gets into a state which is hard to break him out of – no matter what you say or do to try and distract him it's like he's in an irreversible mode. He probably needs a psychiatrist. On a one-to-one basis he is much more obedient. His idea of the centre of the red zone is the vets and his centre of the green zone is the fridge. Bonkers! The red zones are places where he used to go but doesn't want to go there anymore because he's been spooked. He enjoys his daily routines and once the last thing on his menu is gone he throws the towel in and gets grumpy and growly if disturbed.

THE CARNEDDAU

So where does the Carneddau come into this? The peace and tranquility offered by the surroundings are perfect for state of mind of man and dog and much quieter than some better known areas of Snowdonia. The most challenging part of this area is the weather rather than the terrain, with the wind being the main factor. So bad is the wind at times that I have to put the collie back on his lead so he doesn't blow away, even though like most dogs he has a low center of gravity.

Fortunately for him he is not your standard collie, not a working dog, much stockier. He was overweight before we brought him to the Carneddau, but walking thirty to forty miles a week did slim him down a little. When he walks up to Drum in front of me in a spritely manner it reminds me of the nickname I've given him of 'swagger bum'.

Horses 'n cotton buds on saddle betwixt Drum and Foel Fras

For a lot of people — walking to Drum from Aber or Llanfairfechan is more than enough. The views are spectacular enough from there, in good weather. You have to be quite keen to go further to reach peaks such as Dafydd and Clewelyn when starting from the coast. Most people would start out from Llyn Ogwen to reach those two giants.

As a minimum I and the dog walk from LLanfairfechan, up to Drum but our full route takes in Foel Fras, Carnedd Uchaf (old name preferred — stop changing things), Foel Grach and finally Carnedd Llewelyn. Once we even managed to take in Carnedd Dafydd.

I've tried to establish the distances correctly and think it's probably three miles to Drum and six and a half miles to Carnedd Llewelyn. **We always come back the same way we go out,** so you can double the distances to arrive at the overall walk distance of for example; to Drum and back would be six miles and it's fur-teen (doggy) miles to Carnedd Llewelyn and back. Time allowed for the round trips is usually three hours when Drum and allow seven hours to do Carnedd Llewelyn. **I base all our walks on a rate of 2 mph.** It takes this long because sometimes when I turn round to see where the dog is I decide he must have been walking backwards to be that far behind. He is well known for his dawdling and faffing around.

Why are all map elevations now shown in metres? Whose smart (metres) idea was that? No-one can get used to it. Speed limits are still stated in MPH not KPH that's because people cannot relate to the metric system of speed while driving. How would the 'Welsh Three Thousands' fit into it? Would they have to become the 'Welsh One Thousands' — knocking Foel Fras and most of the others off the list?

CLOSE ENCOUNTERS

'Ewe must be having a laugh '

wuffbytes, *'I'm not that interested in the sheep — there are far too many of them, but they do seem interested in me. There is just one who is a bit of a worry to the dogs because she's far too brave to be a sheep. I think she must have got mixed up, maybe someone put her on a lead by mistake and it's gone to her head. Sheep are good tap dancers if you go too close to their lambs.'*

wuffbytes, *'I was dancing once. Crazy horse used to follow me all the way down from windy point to the gate at the Rowen end of what is called a roman road, until he could go no further. He had a strange fascination with me and I could never lose him, he had to be there all of the time. Even when we hadn't been past for a while he still remembered me when the time came. I thought I was bonkers but he is even crazier. I think horses are dogs that have grown too big or they are just thin cows with long faces. Why the long face?'*

Over page: Cisco dancing with crazy horse near windy point, or is he dancing with windy horse near crazy point?

7

DRUM

For anyone who wants a low risk walk with three hours to spare — Drum at 2,526 feet is the ideal destination when approached from the coast. The views from the summit (not guaranteed) are exceptional.

> *The track up to the summit means you shouldn't get lost* and don't really need a map or compass even if the cloud comes down. Make sure you check how windy it's going to be and make sure you understand how this will affect you.*

I and the collie have been up Drum in winter when it was probably ill advised to do so. People were being rescued off there at the time. Nevertheless we continued — only to find the last half mile a real challenge. I'd put the collie back on the lead so he didn't blow away and the snow on the ground was being whipped up into a snow storm. The collie couldn't see because the snow was plastered to his head and body and I had to drag him the rest of the way to the top. I was in danger of losing my wooly hat and if that had blown away I would really have been in trouble, so won't be doing that again*. That cruel, criminal, unforgiving wind.

I wouldn't give in because we were so close to the top. The Collie loves the snow and prances around in it excitedly under calm conditions, but he didn't like what he had been dragged through on that occasion. In these conditions you wouldn't attempt to progress any further since you shouldn't even be on Drum in the first place, unless you are the kind of person who is very experienced and been to the South Pole or climbed Everest.

Then a year later, having not learnt our lesson, we attempted Drum on another bad day. This time everything was fine until we reached around 2,250 feet. Shortly after that point the large track disappeared under thick snow and the cloud came down. Despite great attempts to drag the dog upwards he resisted so that all that was left on the lead was his collar. We had to abandon the walk four hundred yards short of the summit.

That particular day when we didn't make it to Drum

Most times when we set off up to Drum or Foel Fras we end up going further than we intended. Sometimes the weather decides this for us. Sometimes the mood takes us. The dog needs to look in good fettle. We certainly have to have the time. This means we can be under prepared. It takes us so long because he walks at a glacial pace and I'm at a glacial age.

FOEL FRAS

If you want to go further and the conditions and mountain forecast are good then Foel Fras is your next stop and is probably just less than a mile away from Drum. If you are already tired out, and not especially fit, then don't attempt this. There is a long slope from bottom to top which grinds you down, make sure you take plenty of stops on the way up if you start getting out of breath.

The summit of Foel Fras is 3091 feet and you can feel the difference in winter when you are up there. Once you have reached the top you have done all the hard work and getting further along the route is much easier, but time consuming.

☃ The frozen summit of Foel Fras.

Cisco is glad he brought his fur coat.

☺ Safety tip, if you need it.

Further walking advice includes learning to take your next step safely, as the consequences of not doing so are scary. Even when walking with someone else an accident can be challenging, but when on your own you must be even more vigilant. Footwear is very important together with how you take that next step, particularly when the ground is wet. Even the shallowest of slopes can be very slippery with a wet grass and mud combination. Always look to place your foot where there is medium sized gravel, small stones or grass tufts, these drastically reduce the chance of a slip which could put you out of action or end your walking days.

Always be aware of time limitations, particularly in winter so you don't miscalculate and end up in the dark and still be a long way from home.

Our trips pale into insignificance when you come across someone or a group who are in the process of completing all the 'Welsh Three Thousands' or doing the 'Dragons Back Race.' We often meet people on Foel Fras doing the 3000's.

Have there ever been 'We Love Drum', 'We Love Foel Fras' tee-shirts? Were they best sellers? Would you have to donate all proceeds to the Snowdonia National Park? Would you get permission?

How can one best describe all these hills?
They are high with varied inclines. They have rocks, slate, soil, heather, sheep and grass on them. They can be wet or dry, covered in ice, snow or fog. You can sometimes see a long way from them. Why are some of us drawn to climb up them?

FOEL GRACH

If you have the time and have planned things carefully you can proceed a further mile and a half-ish to Foel Grach via Carnedd Uchaf. Foel Grach at 3,202 feet is 111 feet higher than Foel Fras (7 feet lower than Scafell Pike which is 3,209 feet and the highest peak in England). The walk between Fras and Grach is relatively easy, sloping down slightly to Carnedd Uchaf, followed by a further dip after Carnedd Uchaf, rising quite steeply before levelling off towards the refuge hut just before Foel Grach. This is an easy section after the long trek up to Foel Fras. Obviously coming back the same way is much easier than the journey out, but does take its toll on your knees and you are more likely to slip so need to maintain your concentration and take your (well planned) time.

The refuge hut at Foel Grach

CARNEDD LLEWELYN

Carnedd Llewelyn (3,490 feet). When we get to Clewelyn and we are about to set off back I always tell the dog, 'It's all downhill now — apart from the uphill bits'. I'm 'being on the level' with him by saying that. As we all know, 'Clewelyn's' summit is very flat, it must be the largest flat acreage at that level anywhere in Wales or England — might have to check that where Scotland is concerned. You could understand someone calling it Table Mountain. If it's foggy on top and you're not that familiar with it you can easily come off it in the wrong direction due to the number of alternative routes and the hard surface making these routes unclear. A compass is recommended in case of poor visibility. Needless to say, on a clear day, the views are stunning — but not pleasant when it's very windy.

Approach to Carnedd Llewelyn via Foel Grach

Cisco on the roof of the world

Looking across to Carnedd Dafydd from Llewelyn

CARNEDD DAFYDD

Carnedd Dafydd (3,426 feet).Yes, one day we made it all the way to Dafydd from Llanfairfechan. Our first ever visit. This is where all the hills start to get pointy. This will probably be the first and last time the dog makes it to this point. If I get to come again myself it will have to be sooner rather than later. Once again, on a nice day, the views are stunning. It feels like you are higher than Clewelyn, due to the steep slopes all around.

On Carnedd Dafydd with Bethesda to top left.

It's a nice, but in some parts, rocky walk across the ridge from Clewelyn passing the black ladders, staying well away from the edge. You get a good view looking back as you near the top of Dafydd. The full panorama was better than on Clewelyn and Snowdon was a little closer now. We were lucky because the cloud level was quite low. We did 16¾ miles in 8½ hours that perfect day. Well worth the effort. The dog looked chuffed too.

Cisco enjoys a stop for bottled water provided its part of a meal deal. A stuck up tail means he's open for business.

Where your dog v weather is concerned make sure it's not too hot or not too cold. Think of their paws where heat or frost is concerned. Make sure you have water for it, even if it's not a warm day. When it's foggy keep a close eye on the dog, particularly when it's windy, because if you do lose it in the fog chances are it won't hear your call. Any doubts, put it on the lead straight away.

Interesting points — highest peaks comparison (in feet)

<u>Scotland</u>
Ben Nevis	4,411
Ben MacDui	4,295
Braeriach	4,252

<u>Wales</u>
Snowdon	3,560
Crib y Ddysgi	3,494
Carnedd Llewelyn	3,490

<u>The five 3,000's on our walks.</u>
Carnedd Llewelyn	3,490
Carnedd Dafydd	3,426
Foel Grach	3,202
Foel Fras	3,091
Carnedd Uchaf**	3,038

<u>England</u>
Scafell Pike	3,209
Scafell	3,163
Helvellyn	3,119

** See page 27

TREATS

Hopefully humorous — not ridiculous.

We can't let the Collie out on the last Monday in August because it's a Ban Collie Day.

We were nearing home — on our way back from a long walk, when we came across a man. Looking at Cisco and then turning to me he said, 'I'll swap you these three for the dog.' His kids weren't listening to him anyway.

Cisco came second in the 'Naughtiest Dog in North Wales' contest, but who came first — All the other dogs in North Wales.

A Russian Cisco might be called Ciscki Slavachops.

Cisco is misunderstood. He was born at a very early age and probably should have been called Baby-Bel.

One of the few (self-taught) commands he learnt was to respond to the fridge door opening.

Cisco might sip 0.0% wine, smoke a pipe and wear a trilby.

Dogs were reading p-mails long before we were reading emails.

Thirty minutes before treat time he's sat outside the cupboard,
>Dad to Cisco, 'It's not time yet.'
>Cisco to Dad, *'I don't want to be last in the queue'*

At home he's allowed the privilege of jumping onto the settee and sitting next to me. It's like tossing a coin to see whether you get his head or his tail.

How does one outfox a dog?

DOG SCIENCE

Cisco is like a forensic scientist judging by the amount of time he needs to spend analysing a single specimen of something unmentionable. He is not your standard, skinny, working collie — he's longer than normal, more like an articulated, well-built version. He has a slenderness ratio to suit, so that when he is walking perpendicular to a strong side wind he deflects in the middle. Take for example the fence which runs from the gate at Drum generally northwards to what I call windy point (because it hasn't got a name of its own). That fence isn't there to keep in or separate sheep and horses; it's there to catch people, or their dogs who have been blown away, who weren't able to stand up any longer. Then there's his lesson in gravity, when scratching his back on level ground close to a slope, going too close to the edge and then trying to right himself like a cat does as he rolls down the banking.

He's at his happiest when he picks up a stick then prances and canters with it in his mouth like it's an Olympic gold medal, but that special moment never last's long.

DIET

His food must say 'Once open eat within five seconds.' on the label because he eats everything so quickly. Best to hand it to him a little at a time. Exercise requirement to burn off his daily allowance would include a minimum walk of 5 miles per day (35 miles per week) multiple tug of war and ball playing sessions. It's a fine line stopping him from becoming an expanded dog. See his daily menu on next page.

DID ANYONE MENTION FOOD?

oooo Menu oooo

7 am Breakfast

180g of science plan Chicken or Lamb

5 pm Evening Meal

180g of science plan Chicken or Lamb

7 pm Supper

Denture Stick

§

Read the small print
*8 am, 2 little treats. During walk, 2 little treats/hr. Lunchtime, 30g of meat or fish
Dinner, 50g of meat or fish and veg. 8 pm, 2 little treats.*

*T's & C's apply
(Tuna & Chicken)*

THAT WAS THE YEAR THAT WAS

January

The year started slowly with a couple of walks up to Drum in the snow which was drifting off the ground into Cisco's face.

February

We only went on the hills once but made the long icy journey to Clewelyn.

March

We went mad in March and made eleven trips to the hills, five just to Drum, four to Foel Fras via Drum and two to Foel Grach via Drum and Foel Fras. So we were going up every two to three days averaging over 50 miles per week — a feat that would never be repeated. There was an abundance of snow.

April

We couldn't keep up the pace of the previous month and had a good rest with just three trips. Two to Drum and one to Foel Fras via Drum.

May

May saw us get back into our stride — making six trips in total. Four were just to Drum, one was to Foel Fras and the other to Clewelyn.

June

June resulted in six more trips — four just to Drum, one to Clewelyn and one to Foel Fras via Drum. When we reached Foel Fras we went across the saddle to Llwytmor (2785 feet) for the first and up to press, last time. One of the trips to Drum ended with a serious fall coming back down the hill path near home. Needless to say, four legged Cisco wondered why I'd been so clumsy. *'Why don't you walk down on all fours dad?'* He would be thinking. This led to us avoiding our usual return route for nearly six months due to loss of confidence. We would walk back much further by taking the route via Windy hill and crazy horse near Drosgl to the end of the roman road and come back down to LLanfairfechan via Nant-y-Coed. You only need one scary incident to reset your mind around safety.

July

The next month saw much of the same, this time three trips just to Drum with one to Foel Fras and one to Foel Grach via the now all too familiar route. You may ask yourselves why didn't he use his imagination and do something different. Well we did try something different and went to Foel Lwyd via Nant-y-Coed. Foel Lwyd is just short of 2000 feet and is prominent when viewed from the village of LLanfairfechan. When we thought we'd reached the top, just off to the left was another (very rocky) peak close enough to make me think that maybe that was the real summit of Foel Lwyd. We went that little bit further, or so it appeared, and found a way to clamber up only to find when we got back home and looked at the map we had actually been up Tal y Fan which was a separate peak reaching just above 2000. We know our way around so well that we don't take a map out with us. Had we done, we would have realised what we were doing at the time. Notice the use of hyphens in some names and not others like Nant-y-Coed and Tal y Fan.

August

August was a run of the mill month with six further trips, three just to Drum, two to Foel Fras and one to Foel Grach all via the same route there and back.

September

September was special. We only made five trips but one of them was to be the furthest we would ever go. Up to then Carnedd Llewelyn was the furthest we'd ever been from LLanfairfechan or Aber but on this particular day the weather and visibility were perfect. We were both in fine fettle and on reaching Clewelyn we looked across to Carnedd Dafydd and set off determined to get there. For the first time ever we turned Carnedd Llewelyn into just a stopping off point on the way to somewhere else. We hadn't brought rations for such a long journey so the water supply had to be supplemented where it could be by occasional brooks/streams on the way back. That was our greatest ever achievement. On top of that we also managed one trip just to Drum, two to Foel Fras and one to Foel Grach. By October Cisco had lost 7 kg in the last 9 months.

Always be prepared and plan carefully, check the weather forecast before setting out and take appropriate clothing, footwear and water. Be particularly aware during the winter months and don't underestimate the potential ferocity of the weather you might encounter particularly if it is windy and near to or below freezing. Remember you probably won't get a phone signal depending where you are.

October

The long days were getting shorter and we only managed four trips this time, one to Foel Fras and one to Foel Grach. Cisco developed a poorly foot and missed two trips just to Drum later in the month. We are both veterans of Drum.

November

Cisco had to sit out two further trips just to Drum before he came back with a bang when we returned to Carnedd Llewelyn at the end of the month.

December

The year was rounded off with just two trips, both to Foel Fras via Drum completing 54 journeys in total over 52 weeks.

28 to Drum alone
15 to Foel Fras via Drum
6 to Foel Grach via Drum and Foel Fras
4 to Carnedd Llewelyn via the rest
1 to Carnedd Dafydd via Clewelyn and the rest

That meant 54 times to Drum, 26 times to Foel Fras, 11 times to Foel Grach, 5 times to Carnedd Llewelyn (not allowing for return journeys, e.g. passing a peak for the second time on the way back doesn't count.) And 1 trip to Carnedd Dafydd.

wuffbytes, *'Dad tried out a special maneuver once. I didn't know he could move so fast during a semi-reverse summersault. Like some weird acrobatics. And he thinks I behave strange sometimes'.*

ARMIES OF THE CARNEDDAU

Airborne Division

The crows are by far the most prominent and bossy.
They strut around like they own the place.
They would make great undertakers since they know how to deal with the dead.

In old crow folklore half a dozen crows rounded up several hundred seagulls and held them hostage on the hills not far from Drum, only releasing them on the understanding that they acknowledged the superiority of the crow. It's true; I was there and saw the detained gulls. If only I'd taken a photograph.

The crows love to pose for photo shoots on the large stones at the stone circle sites.

Infantry

As guardians of the pathway Sheep are mostly deployed in platoons patrolling the paths and tracks. They normally move away in the same direction you are heading, further up the path, expecting YOU to choose an alternative route. They are mostly unarmed, unless they are from the Ram battalion. They plant pooh mines for people to step on. Said the lamb to the ewe,

'Can you remind me because I'm confused?' 'I can't remember which routes I'm supposed to forget.'

Cavalry.

Horses' plant even bigger pooh mines.
Imagine if the horses were ridden by sheep?
Royal Welsh Mounted Sheep (RWMS) instead of
Royal Canadian Mounted Police (RCMP)
Maybe they wool just fall off.

In winter the infantry and cavalry retreat to the lowlands.

Cisco saying goodbye, with Yr Elen in the background.

Wag more, bark less.

Epilogue

As the years have passed and the red zones have expanded, we don't do what we used to. Walks are more limited. Eventually we might get to a point where the dog won't even go out of the garden. In that memorable year we walked 2,016 miles in total, (taking into account all walks), averaging nearly 39 miles a week for 52 weeks. The year after that we were averaging just about 30 miles a week, 1560 miles in total.

I'll always regret that day when we went to Carnedd Dafydd for not going that little bit further to take in Pen-yr Ole Wen. As for the other 3,000 in the Carneddau we've never made it to, Yr Elen is a bit too much like 'striding edge' for my liking. At my age I'm easily put off.

**Carnedd Uchaf, (although being higher than three of the other 3,000's) is by many not considered to be one of the 3,000's, due to it not having the required relative height gain. Some say there are only fourteen 3,000's, some call Carnedd Uchaf the fifteenth 3,000. So there may only be six of them on the Carneddau.

Dogilogue

'I can't understand mi dad. He was old when he was born but he still wants to try and climb them big hills. I'd prefer to go on a lot of short walks instead of one big one. He has no teeth, no hair and has trouble with wind, particularly on Foel Fras. I put him on the lead; get him hooked up to mi collar and being at the front I show him where to go. I try to get him to have a wee but he's a bit shy and usually waits until no-ones around.'

Acknowledgements

I would like to thank my son Harry for providing the dog. And a thank you to my wife Helen, for her unusually clever contribution of 'Ban Collie Day', which I added to the 'Treats' section.

Every effort has been made to ensure that there have been no copyright infringements within this document. However, if any are identified the author will be pleased to remove them in future editions.

Cisco running a course on social distancing

Printed in Great Britain
by Amazon